NATIONAL GEOGRAPHIC

My Bean Plant

Joseph Ciciano

I can grow a bean plant.
This is what I need:

trowel

soil

gloves

glass jar

seeds

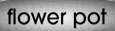

flower pot

watering can

paper towels

3

First, I fold the paper towel and put
it in the jar.

Next, I fill the jar with water.
Then, I put the seeds inside the jar.

Day 7

shoot

root

I check on the seeds.
They are starting to grow.

I can see a root growing from the
bottom of a seed.
I can see a shoot growing from
the top of a seed.

7

Day 14

My bean plant is growing bigger.
I can see the roots growing from
the bottom of the plant.

8

leaves

stem

I can see the long stem.
I can see the leaves.

Day 28

I put my bean plant into a pot.

10

flowers

I water my bean plant.
Little white flowers are growing on
my bean plant.

Day 40

bean pod

Bean pods are growing on my
bean plant.

12

Some of the bean pods are ready
to be picked.

What's inside the pods?
Beans!

beans

Picture Glossary

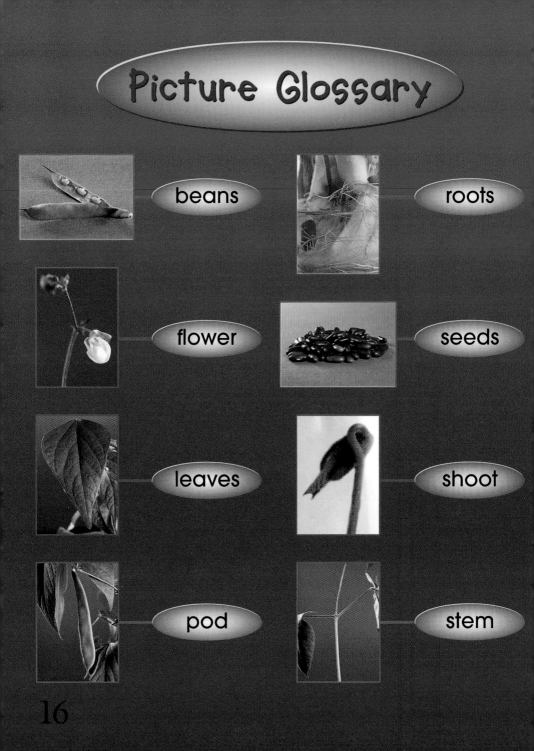

beans

roots

flower

seeds

leaves

shoot

pod

stem